Tell Me a Story

Stories by Maureen Spurgeon
Illustrated by Jane Swift and Stephen Holmes

Brown Watson
ENGLAND

CONTENTS

Penguin's Daydream

Penguin lived at the South Pole. Here, it was always cold, with ice and snow all year round. But Penguin liked sliding on the ice and waddling across the snow. And in the spring, the sun melted some of the ice.

Penguin liked springtime best. That was the time he did lots of swimming, diving into the icy water to catch lots of fish! It was also the time when other birds appeared in the sky, flying around.

One big bird flapped his wings at Penguin.

'Why do you stay on the ground?' it screeched at him.

'Because I cannot fly!' said Penguin.

'You cannot fly?' cried the bird.

The bird flew down and perched on a block of ice. 'So, you have to stay here?' he said to Penguin. 'What a shame! When I think of the places I have seen, flying around the world!' 'Tell me!' said Penguin eagerly.

'I have flown across islands in the south seas!' said the big bird. 'Blue skies, sparkling seas, sunny, warm beaches...' And as the bird talked, Penguin began to see himself, far away from the cold South Pole...

'And the sights in the big cities!' the bird went on. 'So many people walking around, all dressed in splendid clothes! There is always so much to see!'
'Tell me more!' said Penguin.

'Well, the mountains are SO exciting!' said the bird. 'And the sun shines all day long! The sights I have seen!' He looked across at Penguin. 'But why am I telling you all this? YOU cannot fly!'

'No,' said Penguin. 'And YOU cannot swim!' His sharp ears had heard the sound of a ripple beneath the water. He dived in and snapped up a juicy, fat fish in his mouth! What a feast for a hungry Penguin!

The bird looked so longingly at the fish! Then he flew up into the sky, off around the world. Penguin's day-dream had been nice. But, being among the ice and snow and eating a fish all to himself was much nicer!

The Magician

'My magic cabinet!' cried Marvo the magician. He tapped his magic wand against a tall box with a door. 'Who can I make disappear?'

'There's nobody here!' grinned Cola the Clown. 'They've all gone to the Fancy Dress Parade!'

'WE'RE here, Cola!' said Brainy
Brenda. 'Go on, YOU get inside!'
'Oh, thank you!' said Marvo. 'Now, I
close the magic cabinet. I tap the door
with my magic wand! Then, I open the
door! And...'

'Cola's gone!' gasped Brenda.
'Have no fear!' smiled Marvo. 'I close
the cabinet! I tap the door with my
magic wand! I open the door!' But the
cabinet was still empty! Cola was not
there! What were they to do?

'I bet I can find him!' said Brainy Brenda, getting inside the cabinet. 'Shut the door, Marvo!'

'Er, I-I-I tap the door with my magic wand...' stammered Marvo. 'Now, I open the door, and...'

'She's gone!' cried Cheeky Chester.
'Now bring her back!'
'I-I t-tap the door with my wand,' said
Marvo. 'Then, I open the door, and..'
'Still no Brenda!' said Chester. 'What
are you going to do now?'

He began to laugh. 'This is more fun than the Fancy Dress Parade!'
'Cheeky Chester, YOU get inside!' gabbled Marvo. 'You-you'll find a lovely costume for the Parade! Go on!' He pushed Chester inside!

'It's dark in here!' came Chester's voice. 'What's more, I – aaagh!' 'Chester!' cried Marvo. He opened the door. The cabinet was empty. Then he got inside and tapped the floor with his foot...

'Aaaagh!' Marvo fell into a tunnel, swirling towards a ray of sunshine and the sound of voices. 'Marvo!' cried Brainy Brenda. 'So THERE you are!' said Cola.

W-what?' said Marvo. 'W-where?'

'Cheeky Chester wins the Fancy Dress Parade!' came a voice, as – Marvo the Magician!'

'Well!' gasped Marvo, staring at the pointed hat and fine cloak. 'What a WONDERFUL trick!'

Shy Suzy

Suzy was very, very shy! If she tried to read out loud, she went red and her voice faded away! She trembled at the idea of being in a school play. She felt sick at the thought of being on a stage! And now, the Town Carnival was being planned. What was she to do!

'You can be on the school float, Suzy!' said Miss Penn. 'We shall wave to all the people, and...'
'Wave to all the people?' said Suzy, trembling. 'No! No!'
'Join in the singing!' said Mr. Hunt.

'No!' cried Suzy again. 'Everyone will be looking at me!'

'We are going in fancy dress!' said Jane. 'Come and see!' Jane was going as Bo-Peep. She had a blue dress, with a white smock and a toy lamb.

'I'd like to be in fancy dress,' said Suzy, 'but I am scared of seeing so many people and them seeing me.'

'Then I have just the job for you, Suzy!' said Miss Penn. 'A job where nobody will see you at all!'

Jane told the others what Miss Penn had said.

'A job for Suzy?' said Abdul. 'But Suzy is so SHY!'

'A job where nobody will see her?' said Nina. 'That does not make sense!'

It was a lovely day for the Carnival Parade. The school float was decorated with flowers and streamers and the children waved to the crowd.

'Where is Suzy?' asked Abdul. 'I cannot see her!'

'Look, there is Mr. Hunt!' said Nina.
'He is with that lovely, big teddy bear!'
The teddy bear wore a big red bow-tie
and carried a collecting tin. It seemed
everyone wanted to put money inside!
But who was inside the costume?

They followed the bear to the end of the parade.
'Now, who collected all this money for our hospital?' said the mayor. He lifted off the teddy bear's head...
'Suzy!' cried Jane. 'She is not shy!'

'Well, nobody could see me!' said Suzy.
'Only the teddy bear!'
'Now they CAN see you!' said Miss
Penn. 'Do you still feel shy?'
Suzy waved her teddy bear's paw.
'Not shy,' she said. 'Just happy.'

The Lollipop Tree

'Buy my lollipops! My lovely lollipops!
Real fruit lollipops!'

'Oh!' cried Linda. 'Can I please have a
lollipop, Mum?'

'But you have already had a banana
lollipop and an orange lollipop!' said
Mum.

'Well, can I have a strawberry one, now?' said Linda. 'Please!'

'All right!' smiled Mum. 'But this is the last one!'

'One strawberry lollipop!' said the lollipop man.

'You know,' he said, 'you should grow your own lollipop tree!'

'A lollipop tree?' cried Linda.

'Yes!' said the lollipop man. 'Just plant a lollipop stick in the ground and see what happens!'

Mum laughed. But Linda licked on the strawberry lollipop, thinking hard all the time. Then she put the lollipop stick in her pocket. As soon as she got home, she ran out into the garden and began digging.

'You are not going to plant that?' said
Mum. 'The man was only joking about
growing a lollipop tree!'
'I shall try, anyway!' said Linda. She
put the stick into the hole and covered
it over with earth.

Linda watered the spot every day, waiting to see if a lollipop tree would grow. Days went by and nothing happened. 'I told you the man was joking!' said Mum. 'Nobody can grow a lollipop tree!'

'It IS growing!' cried Linda. She pointed at the ground. 'Look! Two little leaves!' Mum was amazed. It was true. Soon, more leaves appeared, then a stalk and a stem.

'My lollipop tree!' said Linda, excited.

'No,' smiled Mum, 'it is not a lollipop tree, Linda! It is a strawberry plant! There must have been strawberry pips on the stick you planted! Those pips are seeds, and now they have grown. What a surprise!'

'That means we shall soon have lots of lovely strawberries!' cried Linda. 'All ready to make some lovely strawberry lollipops! So I did get my lollipop tree, after all!'

'Yes,' smiled Mum. 'You did!'

Teddy Bears' Picnic

Binkie Bear never ever went anywhere without Katy-Jane. 'Fancy bringing HER to our picnic!' said Billy Bear. 'It's for bears, not dolls!'

'Silly old doll!' scoffed Teddy.

'Katy-Jane is NOT silly!' said Binkie. 'She is a CLEVER doll!'

'It's the treasure hunt next!' said Billy. 'THAT's not a game for baby bears and their little dollies!'

'Katy-Jane is a very CLEVER doll!' said Binkie again. But the other bears pretended not to hear.

They wanted to hear all about the treasure hunt from Honey Bear! 'See these paths of paper flowers?' she was saying. 'Well, only one path leads to the treasure! Let us see who can find it first!'

The bears ran off, leaving Binkie alone.
'We'll find the treasure, Katy-Jane!' she
said. 'Let's follow the flowers!'
Binkie picked up one flower, then
another and another, going further into
the woods.

'We must go back soon, Katy-Jane,' she said, 'or... aaagh!' Poor Binkie! With her next step, she felt herself falling, falling...... then landing with a bump! 'Help!' she cried. 'Help!' But there was nobody to hear.

Teddy and Billy Bear had just found the treasure – it was a big box of toys for everyone! But when they had been given out, one toy was left over.

'Who is missing?' said Honey Bear. 'I think it must be Binkie!'

Nobody spoke. But how they all wished they had been kinder to Binkie! They began searching the woods, calling out, 'Binkie! Binkie Bear!' Suddenly, Teddy stopped.

'Look!' he cried. 'It's Katy-Jane!'

'Binkie never goes anywhere without Katy-Jane!' said Teddy. 'She must be somewhere near!'

'Teddy!' came Binkie's voice. 'Teddy Bear, is that you? I have fallen down this hole!'

All the bears helped Honey rescue Binkie! 'Teddy saw Katy-Jane!' said Honey. 'That's how we found you!' Binkie gave her doll a hug.
'I always SAID Katy-Jane was a CLEVER doll!' she cried.

Fixit Fred

Fixit Fred loved fixing things, from a creaky gate to a broken toy! 'I'll fix it!' he said. Trouble was, Fred did not fix anything at all...

'No wonder this gate is stuck!' puffed Billy Baker. 'Fred tried fixing the wobbly handle!'

'Fred fixed a bulb in my lamp!' cried Sally-Jane. 'Now it will not work at all!' 'And that's not all!' said Joe. 'Come and see what Fred has been fixing at school. You just won't believe what a terrible job he has done!'

What a mess they found! Things were sliding off the shelves Fred had put up. There were holes in the walls where he had tried putting pictures up. Doors would not open. Drawers would not close. It was a real disaster!

'I'm off to the football match!' Fred told them. 'I'll wave at the TV cameras, so make sure you are watching!'

'Now,' said Miss Todd when Fred had gone, 'let's try mending some of the things and tidying up after Fixit Fred!'

Outside the sky grew dark and rain beat down. 'You can all stay here until the storm is over,' said Miss Todd. 'Switch on the TV, Sally!'
Fred came in, soaking wet. Rain had stopped the football match!

'Who has been fixing things?' he said.
'Look at those squiggles and dots on
the TV! I'll fix THAT!'
'No, Fred...' cried Sally. 'There is really
no need. You see the TV isn't really
bro........'

'I will fix the indoor aerial!' said Fred.
'Look! The screen is clear!'
'Sorry for the loss of the picture!' said
a voice. 'The bad storm which stopped
today's football match has also
interrupted our programme!'

'We tried to tell you!' said Sally.
'You knew I was trying to fix a TV that did not need fixing?' cried Fred. 'That is the last job I am ever doing!'
'Good!' smiled Miss Todd. 'You can play in the school football team, instead!'

'And help me train my dog!' said Billy.
'And be a clown at all the school
parties!' said Sally.
Fred had to smile! And soon he was so
busy, everyone quite forgot he had ever
been called Fixit Fred at all!

Musical Chairs

Jack was always trying to win something. A coconut at a fair, a prize for the best fancy dress or a cup for coming first in a race, but he had never won anything. Then, he heard about the Musical Chairs Marathon being held at his school.

'People pay money to play musical chairs!' explained his Uncle Sam. 'The money goes to your school! And the winner gets a prize!'

'Let's go in for it, Jack!' said Gary. He was Jack's best friend.

They took some chairs out into Jack's garden. Uncle Sam switched on the radio, and Jack and Gary went round and round the chairs.

'Quick, Jack!' cried Uncle Sam as the music stopped. 'Grab a chair!'

Gary and Jack practised hard, each hoping to win! Then came the day of the marathon, with lots of children in the playground, standing around lots of chairs! Music blared out from loud-speakers and the game began.

The music stopped. Jack sat down at once! The music started up again and round and round they went. The music stopped. Just as Jack grabbed a chair, a girl sat on it! Then he saw some chairs all crowded together.

He ran to the nearest one, ahead of the rest! Again and again, the music began. When the music stopped, Jack got a chair, until the last one was left. And, as the music stopped, he sat down!
'I've won!' he cried.

'The winner of the Musical Chairs Marathon!' said a voice. 'Zita Hill!'

'Zita?' Jack choked. 'But – I won!'

'No, Jack!' said Uncle Sam. 'You have been sitting on chairs that were taken OUT of the game!'

'Well, I'M giving him a prize!' said a lady, feeling in her purse. 'I've never laughed so much!'

'Nor me!' said a man. 'Have a bag of candy for being a good loser!'

Then, Jack began to smile.

'Don't you mind losing, Jack?' asked Uncle Sam.
Jack looked around, proudly clutching his prizes.
'No,' he said, 'I don't mind. I was only practising for the NEXT game of musical chairs!'

Farmyard Surprise

Poppy the shire horse had been at Hill Farm longer than any of the other animals. Big and strong, she pulled the plough, towed wagons piled high with hay, working hard all day. But lately, she did not seem to be quite the same horse as before.

She kept having to stop and rest. Her eyes seemed dull. Her coat looked damp and shiny.

'Poppy can hardly lift her big, shaggy hooves,' said Boxer the dog. 'I do not think she can be very well.'

'Then we must try to make her feel better,' said Shelly Sheep. 'Now, what can we do?'

The animals tried to think.

'What about each of us giving her a present?' said Boxer.

'Good idea!' said Shelly. 'I will give her some of my new fleece! It will make a nice, woolly blanket!'

'And I will give her my bell!' said Candy Cow. 'It will cheer her up to hear it tinkling!'

'I will give her some of my eggs!' said
Hatty Hen. 'All freshly laid today!'
'I will bring her some apples from the
orchard!' said Boxer.
Hopefully the presents would make
Poppy feel better.

But, when they got to Poppy's stable, she was nowhere to be seen.

'Come on, old girl!' they heard the farmer say. 'You will feel better now!' The animals looked at each other. Was Poppy really ill?

Boxer barked. 'We are here, Poppy! Come out and see what we have got for you!'

'No!' came the farmer's voice again. 'You can all come in and see what Poppy has got for YOU!'

They went inside. There was Poppy, looking a bit thinner and rather tired, but her eyes were bright and her coat shone. She was nuzzling her new-born foal, as he took his first, wobbly little steps.

And the presents? Well, Poppy soon ate the apples and the eggs were a real treat for her. But it was Blackie, the baby foal, who slept on the soft, woolly pillow and played with the bell every day after that!

Make A Wish!

'I wish,' said Mandy, 'I really DO wish something nice would happen!' Mum smiled. 'So do I,' she said. Mandy's dad was in hospital and they missed him. 'What would you wish, Mandy?' said her mum. But just as Mandy started to think, the door-bell rang.

It was Mandy's friend, Lucy. She was on her new bike. Lucy let Mandy ride it around the block. The wheels whizzed around and everything seemed to flash past. Mandy was so sorry when it was all over.

'That's what I'd wish for!' she told her
mum. 'A bike of my own!'
'Well, wishing is the only way you will
get a bike!' said Mum.
'We used to wish on dandelion seeds!'
said Mum's friend, Meg.

'Dandelion seeds?' cried Mandy. 'Yes!' said Meg. 'Hold one in your hand, close your eyes, wish hard, then blow on the seed. If it floats away, you get your wish! But you must do it for three days running!'

Mandy could see lots of dandelion seeds floating in the air. It was not so easy to catch one! But, at last, she managed it. She held the seed in her hand, closed her eyes and wished very, very hard.

Then, she blew on the seed and watched it float away. 'I'll get my wish!' said Mandy. Next day, and the day after, she caught a dandelion seed. Each time, she held it in her hand, wished hard and blew!

Next day, Mandy waited for her new bike to appear. She was so sure she would get her wish! But, nothing happened. She started to lose hope. Then, the telephone rang and Mum answered it.

'Hello?' Mandy heard her say. 'Well, how WONDERFUL! Mandy will be so happy when I tell her! She's been wishing hard all week!' Then Mum gave Mandy a kiss! 'Your wish has come true!' she said.

'I – I got my wish?' said Mandy. 'Yes!' said Mum. 'Daddy is coming home from hospital!'

'Daddy is coming home!' Mandy danced around, clapping her hands. 'Yes! That's what I REALLY wished!'

The Ballet Shoes

Tara loved dancing. She often read the story about the princess whose magic shoes made her a wonderful dancer! Then, one day, tucked away in a cupboard, Tara found a pair of old shoes she had never seen before! They fitted perfectly!

Tara wore them to dance at the school concert. She danced better than ever!
'These shoes are MAGIC!' she told herself.
'Tara!' her mum called. 'Fancy you finding my old shoes!'

'YOUR shoes?' said Tara. 'Oh, and I
thought these were magic shoes,
because they made me dance so well!'
'You DID dance well!' said Mum. 'Now
you know that you do not need magic
shoes at all!'

Do you like these stories? Yes?
Now, what comes next?
Well, have a guess!
Lots more stories! Yes, that's true.
And – one about a friend for you.
A jungle friend who looks so bold!
With splendid stripes
Of brown and gold.
And a growl, fierce as can be!
A tall, strong tail! That's right! It's me!
I'm off hunting – come along!
You'll see I'm very brave and strong!

Tiger Cub Goes Hunting

Tiger Cub was bored. Mother Tiger was asleep. There was nothing to do. 'I'm BORED!' he growled. 'I want to go hunting!' It seemed that black and white stripes were moving in the long grass. Was it another tiger? He went to find out.

It took him a long time to follow those black and white stripes!

'But YOU are not a tiger!' said Tiger Cub.

'And YOU are not a zebra!' said Zebra.

'YOU cannot hide your stripes in the long grass!'

'Sssssst….' A long thin body with yellow and black stripes was slithering along the ground.

'YOU are not a tiger!' said Tiger Cub.

'YOU are not a snake!' hissed the snake. 'YOU cannot slither along!'

Next minute, there came a very loud
'R-R-Roar!' Tiger Cub hoped it was
Mother Tiger! Instead, it was an animal
with yellow and gold patches.
'YOU are not a lion!' said the animal.

'YOU are not a tiger!' said Tiger Cub.
'You do not have stripes, like mine!'
'No,' said the lion. 'But I roar the
loudest!' And he gave another roar,
louder this time. 'R-R-ROAR!'

Tiger Cub opened his mouth, ready to roar back. But then there came another roar, louder than both their roars put together!

'R-R-ROAR!' There was no mistaking Mother Lion!

'Mother!' Lion Cub roared back. 'Now we can go hunting!'

'I can hunt, too!' said Tiger Cub. But Mother Lion and Lion Cub were already running off, back into the jungle. Tiger Cub felt a bit sad.

'R-R-ROAR!' Tiger Cub sprang to his feet. He knew that roar, the strong head and the brown and gold stripes! 'Mother!' he cried. 'It IS you!'

'Yes!' said Mother Tiger. 'Tell me, are you still bored?'

'No!' said Tiger Cub. 'I have been watching zebras and snakes and lions! And now I want to go hunting!'

'Then that is what we shall do,' said Mother Tiger. 'Come along.'

The Prize

'I want to win the prize for the biggest turnip at the Garden Show!' Dad told Beth and Joe. 'Will you help me?'
'How can we help?' asked Beth.
'I want you to water the turnip plants each day!' said Dad.

'I grew these turnip plants from seeds!' said Dad. 'Now they are ready to plant out in the garden!'
Beth and Joe watched him putting the little plants in the earth. And next day they started their work!

First, they filled a watering can from the tap. Some water slopped onto the ground. 'Careful, Beth!' said Joe. Too late! Beth slipped on the wet patch and fell down, squashing a whole row of turnips as she fell!

Beth was not hurt. She was more
worried about the turnips! 'I saw some
more plants in the greenhouse!' said
Joe. He fetched a box of plants and
they put them into the earth, just like
Dad had done.

When Dad saw the row of new plants
and heard what happened, he laughed!
'Well,' he said, 'if your turnips grow
half as big as mine, YOU'LL win a
prize at the Show!' And off he went,
still laughing!

Beth and Joe were very excited! 'Could we win a prize?' said Beth. 'Our turnips do look a bit small...'
'Only because we planted ours after Dad's,' said Joe. 'Let's try and do our best, anyway!'

All the plants grew big and strong. Then the time came to dig up the turnips! And what fine, big turnips they were! Dad was very pleased!
'Your turn!' he told Beth and Joe. 'Let's see what yours are like!'

They dug carefully. 'Oh,' said Beth, 'ours are not so big and round.'
'But Dad said we could win a prize if ours were half as big as his turnips!' said Joe. 'And they are!'
'Right!' said Dad. 'Let's go!'

Well, Dad DID win the prize for the biggest turnip! Beth and Joe won a prize, too – for the biggest RADISHES! 'I was going to grow them!' said Dad. 'But now I shall leave the radish-growing to YOU!'

Daisy Doll

Daisy was a beautiful doll with beautiful blue eyes, beautiful hair and beautiful clothes. So it came as no surprise when the teddy bears asked her to sing at their picnic.

'I shall wear my frilly pink dress with a bow in my hair!' she cried.

Wooden Wendy was watching.
'You poor thing Wooden Wendy!' said
Daisy. 'You have nothing beautiful to
wear! Never mind! You can help me get
ready! Now, what song shall I sing to
begin with?'

'Teddy Bears Come Out To Play? Or
perhaps... Sing a Song of Teddy Bears?
Or what about Teddy Bear, Teddy Bear,
Where Have You Been? Do you know
that one, Wendy?'
Wendy looked up at Daisy.

'No,' said Wendy in a small voice.
'I shall teach you!' smiled Daisy. She
cleared her throat and began. 'Teddy
Bear, Teddy Bear, where have you
been? I've been to the park where it's
all nice and green!'

On and on, Daisy sang and sang in her high, wobbly sort of voice, over and over again. By the time she had finished, Wooden Wendy knew every, single word of every, single song!
But, what a terrible noise!

'I am glad it is the Teddy Bears' Picnic tomorrow!' said Piggy Bank. 'I cannot stand much more of Daisy and her singing!' The toys agreed. But Daisy did not hear. She was already in bed, fast asleep!

Next day, Daisy was glad to see that the
sun was shining.

'What a lovely day for the picnic!' said
teddy. Then, Daisy opened her mouth
to sing – but no sound came out. After
so much singing, she had lost her voice!

'Lost her voice?' said Rabbit. 'So, who is going to sing at the picnic?'
'Why not ask Wooden Wendy!' cried Piggy Bank. 'She knows all the songs! And Fairy Doll will lend her a dress and a crown!'

Well! Wearing a pretty dress and a crown, Wendy looked beautiful!

'Do come to the picnic, Daisy,' she said. 'Voice or no voice, you can still have a lovely time with the rest of us!'

And, they did!

The Little Digger

Del was a little digger. Bigger diggers dug roads and canals and motorways. Del did the little jobs, like digging goldfish ponds and flower beds. But sometimes he wished that he did the same work as the bigger diggers!

'But you move quicker than the bigger diggers, Del!' said Ben, his driver. 'And you can turn around in a small space! Wait until we start the next job! Then you will see just how important you really are!'

Del winked his headlights. Just suppose the next job was on the motorway! Or digging a big road! But Ben drove him into a flat space, away from the main road. 'Here we are, Del!' said Ben. 'Start digging!'

First, Del dug a shallow, round hole.
Then he dug a long, deep trench.
'Some children are watching!' said Ben,
as Del started digging another hole.
The children cheered and waved.

Del winked his headlights.
'Why are they cheering me?' he asked
Ben. 'I am only a little digger!'
'But you are a nice little digger!' said
Ben. 'And you work hard. That is why
they like you!'

'Time to dig another hole,' said Ben,
'and then a ditch. This has been a great
little job, Del!'
Del was not too sure about that! What
was the good of holes and ditches and
a trench in the middle of a flat space?

'Just one flower bed!' Ben said next day. 'Then we are finished, Del!' But, as they went along, all the children clapped and cheered! Then, Del saw a lovely sandpit and a big paddling pool.

A rocking horse was fixed in one ditch and where there had been another hole, there was now a little drinking fountain!

'It is a new children's playground!' said Ben. 'And you did all the digging, Del!'

'Del!' cried the children in the sandpit, the paddling pool, on the rocking horse and at the fountain. 'Hurrah for Del the Digger!' Del winked his headlights. Being a little digger WAS important, after all!

The Magic Carpet

Mark knew the story of Aladdin by heart! He loved hearing how he rubbed his magic lamp and how the genie granted his wishes. But, best of all, Mark liked the part about Aladdin flying swiftly across the sky on his wonderful magic carpet!

His Dad even let Mark choose an Aladdin sort of rug for his bedroom! It had stars, a moon and fluffy clouds in a deep blue sky.

'My own magic carpet!' said Mark. 'Just like Aladdin!'

Mark closed his eyes. He could almost feel himself flying through the air – until he opened his eyes and saw he was still in his own bedroom. Then, Mark remembered! Aladdin only flew on his magic carpet at night!

Mark waited until it was quite dark. Then he sat on the rug and closed his eyes tight. He felt a breeze, becoming light and warm. The rug rippled beneath him. Then he opened his eyes wide...

He was flying above towns, then over
mountains with clouds brushing against
his hair! All at once, the sky became
blue and the sun shone down on a
sandy beach.

'I wish we could land!' he cried.

Next minute, he was on the sand, palm trees waving in the breeze! But it felt very quiet and lonely. Mark did not like it much. At last, he sat on his magic carpet, wishing he knew how to make it move.

A cloud blotted out the sun. Mark clutched at his magic carpet, trying to lift it up. Now, a whirlwind was swirling around, making Mark shut his eyes tight. 'I want to go home!' he cried. 'I want to go home!'

Mark felt himself twirling, then swirling.
Then – BUMP! Where was he, now?
'Mark!' Someone was calling his name.
'Mark!' said Dad. 'I thought I heard a
bump! Did you fall out of bed!'

Mark shook his head and climbed into bed. Flying on a magic carpet had been exciting, but perhaps he would wait a little while before trying it again. He turned over and went fast asleep.

The Railway Coach

Tim had been given a train set on his sixth birthday. It had a signal, tracks to lay out on the floor, a red engine to pull the train, trucks for goods and one lovely, blue passenger coach. Tim liked the passenger coach best of all.

Tim liked to slide the roof off the coach. Then he was able to reach inside and feel the soft seats. The little tables had a tiny lamp on them. But he wished he had passengers to ride inside the coach!

Time passed. Tim grew up. Now, the
coach was dented and the doors were
hanging off.
'What can we do with this old thing?'
he asked his girlfriend. 'Do you think it
is any use to anyone?'

'Put it in this box of things for the jumble sale,' said his girlfriend. 'Someone may buy it.'

'But it has no wheels!' said Tim. 'Still, I suppose you never know! Come along, we must be going!'

Tim and his girlfriend sold lots of things at the jumble sale. But nobody wanted the old passenger coach.

'You know,' said Tim, 'when I was a boy, I always wished I had some passengers to go inside!'

A lady and a girl were close by. 'No good you hoping for a dolls' house, Amy!' the lady was saying. 'Besides, where could we keep it?'

Amy pointed at the coach. 'What is that over there?' she asked.

'This?' smiled Tim. 'It is only an old passenger coach!'

'Look!' cried Amy. 'It has tables with lamps and seats which fold down to make little beds! It will make a lovely house for my dolls!'

'And we can certainly find room for it in our little home!' said Mummy.

'And I ALWAYS wanted to see passengers in that coach!' said Tim.

Amy smiled. She couldn't wait to get the coach home.

Very soon the old coach was looking almost as good as new! It still had no wheels, but Amy didn't mind. After all, with her dolls living inside, it was not going anywhere, anymore. But what a lovely home it made for them!

Hidden Treasure

Jay lived by the sea at Sandy Bay. His Uncle Dan often told him that Sandy Bay was the place where a ship, belonging to Greybeard the Pirate, had been wrecked, many, many years ago. Again and again, Dan had tried to find the wreck.

One night, there was a great storm.
Thunder rolled and winds whipped up
high waves, crashing them onto the
shore. Next day, the damage was plain
to see. Tiles had been torn from roofs,
fences blown down.

'There's some wreckage in the sea, Mike!' Uncle Dan told Jay's Dad. 'That storm must have disturbed the wreck of Greybeard's ship! Get the boat out! Jay, fetch your life-jacket! Let's see if there is any sign of the treasure!'

Soon, Jay was in the cabin of Dan's boat. Dad stayed on deck.

'Look!' cried Dan, pointing. 'Timber from the ship!' He got ready to dive. 'Keep an eye on that computer screen, Jay!' said Dan. 'You'll see it all!'

There was a splash and Dan had gone. Jay kept watching the screen. Then he saw Dan moving towards the dark shape of the wreck, and – something shining in the water, like sunbeams! But it was not the Sun.

'Treasure!' gasped Jay, his eyes looking at a very old chest with fish and sea horses darting in and out. A baby octopus was curled up inside a crown and tiny crabs scuttled around happily inside a silver cup.

Jay held his breath.

'Please, Uncle Dan,' he whispered, 'leave the chest for the fish and the sea horses and the crabs and the octopus!' But next minute, the treasure chest disappeared in a cloud of sand!

Little by little, the sand began to settle at the bottom of the sea. Jay saw lots of fish and sea horses darting in and out of the chest, an octopus inside a crown, and tiny crabs scuttling around a silver cup!

'Mike!' came Dan's voice. 'I'm bringing up a brass name-plate, an anchor and a cannon! Not bad, eh?'

'No treasure, Dan?' asked Dad.

'Treasure?' said Dan, winking at Jay. 'This is enough treasure for me!'

On Safari!

Paul and his dad had come to spend a day at the big Safari Park! Here, elephants, zebras, monkeys and lots more animals roamed around instead of being locked up in cages. Paul had packed a whole bag of treats for them all. He was very excited!

Paul had some sunflower seeds to give to the parrots. But first, he wanted to help feed the elephants! He held out a bun and a baby elephant came up to him, trunk waving. People began to smile at him.

Next, Paul went to see some donkeys, feeding them carrots and apples. 'Come and see this boy!' someone called. 'All the animals seem to know him!' Lots of people began to follow Paul about.

Some took photographs. Paul felt quite proud! He liked hearing them talking and laughing. Then he remembered the sunflower seeds he had got for the parrots. He went and put some in their feeding pots.

'Ha-ha!' someone laughed. 'Look at him now!' Paul held out some more seeds. But no parrots came.
'Ha-Ha!' they laughed again. Paul scowled. What was so funny?

'Ha-ha!' people laughed. 'Ha-ha!' By now Paul was very angry! No wonder the parrots would not feed, with all the noise going on. Then there was a tap on Paul's shoulder. He turned round, still angry.

Two big paws gave him a push!
'Chico!' came a man's voice. 'There
you are! Bad chimp!'
But Chico the chimp was busy eating
fruit from Paul's bag!
'I thought he was lost!' said the man.

'Not while he was following my Paul around the zoo!' said Paul's dad. 'The funny thing was, Paul did not know about it!'

'No,' grinned Paul. He gave Chico a banana. 'No, I didn't!'

'Thanks for looking after Chico, Paul!' said the man. 'How would you like an ice cream, as a reward?'
'Thank you,' said Paul. 'And, can I take my friend Chico for a walk, as well?'

Sam and Candy

Sam the dog and Candy the cat lived in Ernie's shop. Ernie sold lots of things like nails, screws, hammers, paintbrushes and gardening tools. Sam helped Ernie to look after the shop. Candy kept busy, chasing away mice and spiders.

As soon as anyone came into the shop, it was – 'Hello there, Sam! Good dog!' or 'How is Sam today?' But nobody said anything about Candy.

'I work hard, like you!' she said to Sam. 'Yet nobody notices me!'

'I am more important!' said Sam.
'Ernie needs me to chase robbers!'
'What robbers?' asked Candy. But Sam
was already running off, barking. Sue
Sharp was in the shop with her new
dog, Pickle!

'Pickle is a fine little dog!' cried Ernie.
'What do you think, Bill?'
'I think he wants me to throw him my
old wooden ruler!' said Bill. 'I have had
it since I was a boy! Can I buy a new
one just like it, Ernie?'

He held up the ruler to show Ernie.
Sam barked. 'All right, Sam!' said
Ernie. 'Bill is only showing me his
ruler!' Sam barked again. Pickle barked
back. 'All right, boy!' grinned Sue. Bill
smiled, too.

Bill put down the ruler – and Pickle
grabbed it in his mouth!

'No, Pickle!' cried Sue. She tried to get
the ruler back. But Pickle backed away
and ran off around the corner! 'My
ruler!' cried Bill.

'He's squeezing under the fence!' cried
Ernie. 'Sam is too big to chase after
him now!' Just then, something brown
and furry streaked past Sam! It was
Candy, joining in the chase! She soon
squeezed under the fence!

The fur rose on her back and she hissed and snarled. Pickle barked back – and dropped Bill's ruler! He was still barking and Candy was still hissing when Ernie and Sue got there – just in time!

'Good cat, Candy!' said Ernie. He picked up the ruler. 'You made Pickle drop that ruler and got it back for Bill! What a clever cat!'
Even Sam gave a loud bark to show that he quite agreed!

Rainy Day Picnic

It was the day of the school picnic. Just as the children arrived in the woods, it began to rain. 'The birds love the rain!' said Miss Hill. 'Look at them splashing about and chasing leaves across the puddles!'

That gave Suzy an idea. 'Let's race paper boats!' she said.

They were still ·sailing boats and jumping puddles, when the sun came out again. How fresh the woods felt! And how cool all their food was!

'A rainbow!' cried Cindy. 'Let's make a wish, quickly!'

'I LOVE rainy day picnics!' said Guy, biting into a sandwich. And, the birds? They sang and whistled as if they quite agreed with him!

Time to go
And say goodbye!
But there's more fun –
I'll tell you why!

Just turn the pages
Back, and then –
Enjoy the stories
Again and again!

This edition first published in 2002 by
Brown Watson
The Old Mill, 76 Fleckney Road,
Kibworth Beauchamp,
Leicester LE8 OHG.

Reprinted 2003, 2004, 2005, 2006

ISBN 0-7097-1436-X

Printed in Egypt